# JULIANA

# JULIANA

ROSANA NAVARRO
MARGARITA PÉREZ GARCÍA

English translation and adaptation by
ANNY EWING, TERRY WALTZ
& JUDITH LOGSDON-DUBOIS

Juliana (English)
English translation and adaptation by
Anny Ewing, Terry Waltz & Judith Logsdon-Dubois

Translated with permission of the copyright holders.

Copyright
Originally published in Spanish under the title Juliana,
in January 2018, in Wellington, New Zealand.
© 2018 Rosana Navarro and Margarita Pérez García.

All rights reserved.
No part of this publication may be reproduced, stored in
a retrieval system, or transmitted, in any form or by any
means (electronic, mechanical, photocopying, recording
or otherwise), without the prior written permission from
Rosana Navarro & Margarita Pérez García.

Book design © 2018 Margarita Pérez García
Illustrations © 2018 Avoltha
Cover illustration © 2018 Avoltha
Cover design © 2018 Les Solot

ISBN-13: 978-0-9951215-0-8
A catalogue record of this book is available
from the National Library of New Zealand.

First published by in New Zealand in April 2019

> "I have no special talent.
> I am only passionately curious."
> —Albert Einstein.

# CONTENTS

| | |
|---|---:|
| Characters | 8 |
| Cave | 13 |
| Tunnel | 16 |
| Light | 20 |
| Trapped | 24 |
| Microchip | 26 |
| Danger | 30 |
| Vampires | 34 |
| Explosives | 42 |
| Idea | 46 |
| Juliana's Cave | 50 |
| Glossary | 54 |
| Thanks | 60 |

# CHARACTERS

Juliana is not a typical bat. Juliana is white. Juliana is an albino bat. She is special. Juliana hears everything... She is very curious. And she has excellent ideas.

Juliana has a brother. His name is Shadow. Shadow is not a white bat. Shadow is small and black. Shadow is very curious.

Merlin is a big bat. He is intelligent and the other bats listen to him.

Mr. Rich is rich. He has money, but he has a problem. Mr. Rich wants more money.

Salvador doesn't have a problem. He has a dog. His dog's name is Einstein. Einstein is very intelligent.

## one
# CAVE

In Spain, there is a very special cave. It's a big, black cave. There are a lot of animals in the cave. There are a lot of bats.

It's daytime. There is total silence in the black cave. The bats are sleeping. All the bats are sleeping in silence.

Suddenly, there is a noise.

# Boom, grrrakka kkakkakkakka!

It's a horrible noise. In the black cave, a white bat opens her eyes. It's Juliana, the albino bat.

Juliana opens her eyes: two red eyes in the black cave. Juliana looks towards one part of the cave. She looks towards another part of the cave. She looks at the other bats. They are all sleeping.

She...is not.

Juliana isn't sleeping.

She's listening to the horrible noise.

# Boom, grrrakka kkakkakkakka!

*Again? Not again! Oh no!* Juliana thinks.

Juliana is anxious. She looks at the other bats. She thinks about the differences between them: The other bats don't hear the noise, but Juliana does. The other bats are sleeping, but Juliana isn't. The others are black. She's white. Juliana is white and she has red eyes. She is an albino. She is the albino bat.

The other bats aren't different…

Juliana is!

# Boom, grrrakka kkakkakkakka!

*What's that noise? Is it an animal?* Juliana is listening to the horrible noise. She is not sleeping.

*Why is everyone sleeping, and I'm not?*

# two

# TUNNEL

It's a big noise now.

## Kkakkakkakka! Boom! Boom!

*There's a problem*, Juliana thinks. *There are a lot of animals in the cave. But that noise isn't an animal noise. It's a different noise. It is not a typical cave noise.*

Juliana is curious. Juliana wants to know what the noise is. And Juliana has an idea. There is a tunnel in the cave. It is a big, black tunnel. Juliana looks at the tunnel and listens carefully. The noise is in the tunnel! So Juliana flies towards the tunnel. Juliana flies silently.

In the cave, another bat opens his eyes. It's Shadow, Juliana's brother. Shadow isn't sleeping. He's curious, and he has an idea.

Black like the black cave, Shadow flies silently towards Juliana.

"Juliana, do you have an idea? Another idea?" says Shadow curiously.

"Shhhhh! Go to sleep!" Juliana says anxiously.

"What's your idea?" says her brother.

"You're a small bat," Juliana says to him. "It's not your problem! Go to sleep!" And Juliana flies towards the tunnel.

*Small?* Shadow thinks angrily. Shadow is very curious, so he flies silently behind Juliana.

Now Juliana is in the tunnel... everything in front of her is black. Everything behind her is black too. Now it's a very big noise!

# Boom, grrrakka kkakkakkakka! Booooom! Booooom!

Juliana listens carefully...

But there's another noise. What is it? Is it Shadow?

Yes, it's Shadow! He is in the tunnel too. Now Juliana is very angry. So she flies towards Shadow. She flies fast...

Suddenly there is an explosion.

# Boooooom!

"Juliaaaaaaaaaaana!"

"Shaaaaaaaadow!"

Are they trapped?

 ## three
# Light

There are rocks everywhere. Rocks, rocks, and more rocks. The tunnel is black. Suddenly, there's a light. It's a bright light. Excellent! They are not trapped. Juliana and Shadow fly towards the bright light. They don't fly towards the cave. They fly towards the bright light and the horrible noise.

Juliana listens and looks towards the noise.

It's not an animal. It's a big metal machine.

And it's not one machine. There are two! Three! Four! There are a lot of big machines: big yellow monsters with bright white eyes.

Juliana and Shadow look towards the mountain. It's a construction area with people and machines everywhere.

## It's horrible!

Juliana looks towards the light. But Juliana has a problem. The light is very bright. And Juliana can't see very well, so she thinks fast.

"Shadow, I have an excellent idea!" says Juliana.

Shadow listens carefully.

"You can see very well. Fly between the monsters. Fly fast towards the other tunnel in the mountain," Juliana says to Shadow.

"What about you? You can't see well!" Shadow says to her.

"No problem. You fly in front and I will fly behind you," Juliana says to him.

So Shadow flies between the metal monsters. He flies towards the mountain. He flies fast. But Juliana can't see well, and she doesn't fly behind Shadow. Juliana flies towards the bright light. And she flies into one of the metal machines!

Suddenly, everything is black.

## four
# TRAPPED

It is the end of the day. There is a lot of activity in the construction area. But it's not the machines. It's a dog. It's Einstein.

Einstein is not a typical dog. He is a very special dog. He is a very intelligent dog, and he runs very fast. Einstein runs all day. He runs around the construction area and all around the mountain too.

He is a very curious dog.

Suddenly, Einstein stops running. He looks carefully at the metal machines. Einstein can see two animals. One is black and one is white. The black animal is flying in front of the white one, between the machines. It is flying fast towards the mountain. The white animal is flying behind. It doesn't fly between the machines. It flies towards the bright light. And it flies into one of the metal machines!

Einstein runs fast towards the white animal, but it isn't moving.

The white animal doesn't open its eyes…

Einstein thinks fast. He thinks about the big animals on the mountain at night. The night is dangerous for small animals. Then Einstein opens his big mouth. He takes the white animal in his mouth and runs.

Shadow is behind a rock on the mountain. Juliana is not behind him. Shadow looks towards the construction area. There are people everywhere, but Juliana isn't there. Shadow looks more carefully...

Oh no!

Juliana is in a dog's mouth!

# "Nooooo!"

## five
# MICROCHIP

Einstein runs with Juliana in his mouth. He runs towards a man, fast. The man is Salvador, an engineer in the construction area.

"Einstein! What do you have in your mouth? What is it? It's an animal…" Salvador says. He looks carefully. "It's a bat!"

Einstein opens his mouth. Salvador takes the white bat. Einstein is angry: Grrrr!

A horrible man is walking towards Salvador. It's Mr. Rich, the construction manager. Mr. Rich looks at Einstein. He's angry. Mr. Rich looks at Salvador. He looks at the white animal in Salvador's hands.

"Is there a problem?" says Mr. Rich.

"Yes, there's a problem! There is a bat in the construction area! And if there is one bat, there are a lots of bats. There is a cave in the mountain. There is a colony of bats in the cave." says Salvador.

"That's not my problem. So there is no problem," says Mr. Rich.

"B-b-but we have to stop building the highway," says Salvador, anxiously.

"What? Stop building the highway?" says Mr. Rich. He is very angry.

"No, Salvador. Time is money! There's no time!"

# "Yes, there is! I need one day! I will see if there are more bats," Salvador says to him.

"One day, Salvador. You have one day. No more. If there are no more bats, then the highway construction will not stop. Time is money!"

Mr. Rich walks back to the construction area. He walks fast. He's not thinking about the animals. He's thinking about money.

Salvador walks towards the laboratory. He is thinking about the animals and he has an idea. Salvador wants to know where the bats are. Salvador wants to know where the cave is. Salvador thinks about the machines. He thinks about the explosions. The bat colony is in danger!

Salvador thinks about the white bat…

If the white bat has a microchip, I can see where it goes. If the white bat goes to the cave, I can see where the cave is.

Juliana opens her eyes. Salvador is walking towards Juliana. He has a microchip in his hand.

# "Nooooooooo!"

## six
# DANGER

Shadow flies towards a tunnel. In the tunnel, everything is black. There are rocks everywhere. There are big rocks and small rocks. There are a lot of rocks. Shadow can't fly between the rocks.

*No problem! There's another tunnel*, Shadow thinks.

Shadow flies towards the other tunnel. He flies fast. There are a lot of rocks there, too. But there are very small spaces between the rocks. So Shadow flies carefully between the rocks.

The cave is at the end of the tunnel. Excellent! But everything is in chaos in the cave. It is total chaos. The bats aren't sleeping. They are flying around everywhere. They fly towards the tunnels. But it's impossible. There are a lot of rocks. The bats are trapped in the cave.

## It's horrible!

Shadow flies fast towards a big bat and says to him: "Merlin! Merlin! There's a problem! We are trapped! There's a construction area on the mountain! There are people everywhere!

"Silence!" says Merlin and all the bats stop and listen. They look at Merlin in total silence. "What about Juliana? Where is your sister?"

"Juliana is there, in the construction area!" Shadow says.

"What?" says Merlin.

Shadow hears the other bats in the colony:

"Juliana?" a bat says.

"Who is Juliana?" another bat says.

"The albino bat. The horrible one," says another.

"Yes, the one who is different," says a bat.

"Juliana? She's not important! We are more important!" everyone says.

"Silence!" says Merlin angrily. "White? Black? We are all important!"

Merlin looks at all the bats in the colony. He is anxious. All the bats look at Merlin in silence.

Merlin thinks: *We are trapped. It is the end of the colony.* He says,

"We need an idea."

"Yes! We need Juliana!" says Shadow. "Juliana has a lot of ideas. Her ideas are excellent!"

"Shadow, fly towards Juliana. Fly fast! You are small and you are not trapped. Fly to Juliana."

Shadow flies towards Juliana.
There is total silence in the cave.

## seven
# VAMPIRES

It is night. Juliana is not with Salvador. She is on a rock in front of the tunnel. But she is not flying. Juliana is thinking: *I have a microchip now. If I fly to the cave, the man can see where I'm going. But the cave is secret. There are no people in the cave. No! I will not fly!*

Then Juliana thinks about the explosions: *But I need to see Merlin. Merlin needs to know there is a problem. The colony is in danger! Do I fly, or not?*

Then she hears…

"Juliana! Juliana! Fly fast! Everyone is trapped. We need an idea!" Shadow says.

Juliana thinks fast.

"Let's go! I have an idea. Fly fast! Fly fast!"

Juliana flies towards the construction area. Shadow flies behind her. Juliana and Shadow fly to Einstein. But the dog is sleeping. The two bats open their mouths. They open their mouths like vampires and say:

Eeeeeeeeeeeeeeeeeeeeeee

It's a horrible noise! Einstein opens his eyes.

Grrrrr! And he runs after the bats.

The two bats fly very fast. Now they are flying towards Salvador. But Salvador is sleeping. So the two bats open their mouths. They open their mouths like vampires and say:

Eeeeeeeeeeeeeeeeeeeeee
It's a horrible noise!

Salvador opens his eyes. "Nooooooo!"

Then Juliana and Shadow fly towards the tunnel. Einstein runs after them. Salvador runs after them with a bright light. Einstein and Salvador run fast towards the tunnel.

Salvador can see the tunnel. Juliana and Shadow stop flying. Salvador can see the rocks. There are rocks everywhere. It's horrible.

*There is a cave behind the rocks. There is a colony of bats. They are trapped!* Salvador thinks.

Then Salvador runs fast to the construction area. Einstein goes with him. He runs fast too.

"Juliana," Shadow says to her angrily.

"Your idea is no good!"

## eight
# EXPLOSIVES

Mr. Rich is in the construction area. He looks towards the mountain and thinks: *One day, Salvador. You have one day. Then the construction goes faster, with more explosions. Time is money!*

Salvador runs back to the tunnel. He runs faster. He has two explosives. He thinks about Mr. Rich. *Time is money!*

In the tunnel, there are rocks everywhere. But that's not a problem for Salvador. Salvador has two small explosives. Juliana and Shadow see the explosives. They are anxious.

"One, two, three…" says Salvador. There's an explosion.

# Booooom!

Everyone in the construction area hears the explosion.

It's a small explosion, but Mr. Rich thinks: *Excellent! Time is money!*

Juliana and Shadow can see the rocks moving. Salvador is in the tunnel! Salvador opens the tunnel with the explosives and says:

"Fast! There are no rocks now. Let's go!"

The bats fly in. Salvador and Einstein run after them. Salvador runs to the cave. He can see the bat colony. The bats can see Salvador, too.

But Salvador has a problem. Salvador is thinking about Mr. Rich. There is no more time. The highway will not stop. The explosions will not stop. The machines will not stop.

The bat colony is in danger!

Then Juliana has an excellent idea. All the bats in the cave fly to the machines.

Everyone in the construction area hears a horrible noise!

# Eeeeeeeeeeeeeeeeeeeee

Suddenly, there are a lot of bats. It is daytime, but everything is black, because there are a lot of bats. Mr. Rich sees the bats. He thinks: *That's impossible!*

All the bats fly to Mr. Rich.

And Einstein runs behind them. Grrrrr!

"Neooooooo!"

## nine

# IDEAS

The officials visit the construction area. They say: "There's a problem. There is a cave and there is a bat colony on the mountain."

"Yes. The bats are more important than the highway," says Salvador. "We need a good idea to protect the bats."

So, the officials stop the highway construction for two or three days. The bats are in danger because of the construction. All the animals are in danger. So Salvador is thinking about the problem. Now he has time to think.

Salvador thinks about the bats: *There are a lot of cars on the highway. At night, the cars have bright white lights. Bats fly to bright lights at night. And they fly into the cars. That's a problem.*

Salvador thinks about the other animals on the mountain: *There are a lot of cars on the highway. Animals run day and night. They run on the highway. And they run into the cars. All the animals are in danger because of the highway.*

Salvador has an idea. It's an excellent idea. They build four special tunnels for the animals. The tunnels are animal highways! There is a wall too. It is a metal wall. The walls protect the bats at night. Now the bats are not in danger.

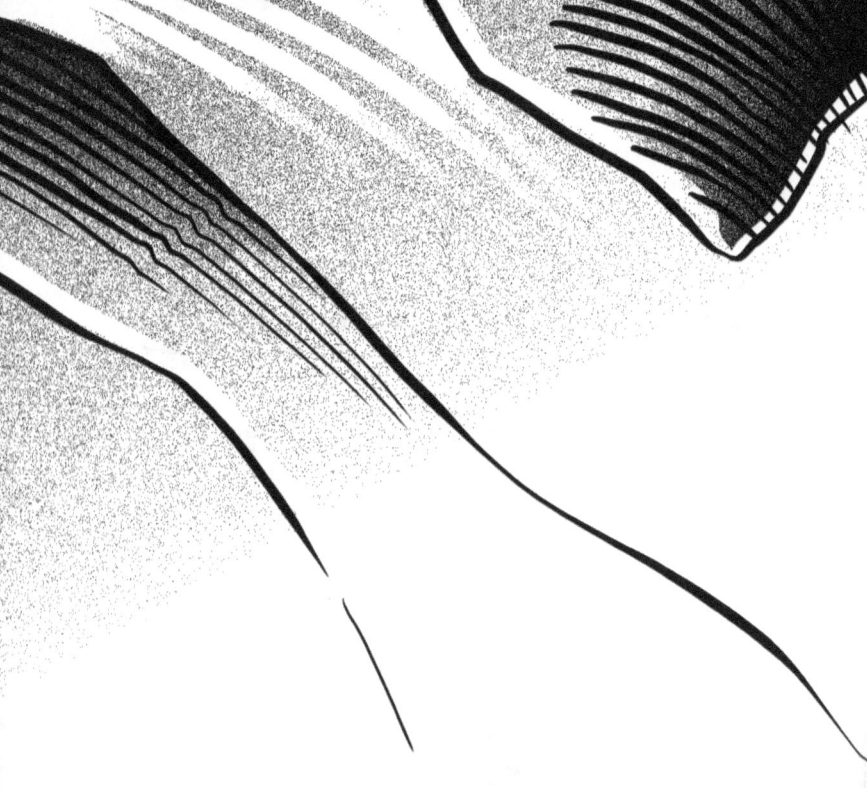

"Let's go, Shadow! Fly fast!" says Juliana.
"Another idea?" Shadow says curiously.

"Yes. Let's fly to the special tunnels! There's a noise, and I want to know what it is..."

"Again?" says Shadow curiously. "Yes, but now you fly in front."

# epilogue
# JULIANA'S CAVE

The story of Juliana and Shadow is fiction. But the story of the cave and the highway is not fiction. It is real. In Spain, in Alicante, there is a very special cave. It is Juliana's Cave.

Juliana's Cave is a special cave because there are a lot of animals in it, especially bats. There are six different bat colonies. There are more than 1,850 bats.

# That's a lot of bats!

In 2011, the Mediterranean Highway was built in Spain. It is Highway A7. The highway goes between Barcelona and Algeciras. But there was a problem. They needed more time for the highway construction, because there were a lot of bats on the mountain. They needed to protect the bats. The bats were more important than the highway!

So, the engineers had a good idea. They built four special tunnels for the animals. The tunnels are animal highways.

There is a wall too. It is a metal wall. The walls protect the bats at night. So the bats are not in danger and they can fly on the mountain. They don't fly into the bright lights of the cars. It is an excellent idea.

# GLOSSARY

Create your own glossary using this list of words. Download the glossary in editable format from the Facebook page *The story of Juliana* and add the definitions in your preferred language.

**A**

a -
about -
activity -
after -
again -
albino -
Algeciras -
Alicante -
all -
an -
and -
angrily -
angry -
animal -
animals -
another -
anxious -
anxiously -
are -
area -
aren't -
around -
at -

**B**

back -
Barcelona -
bat -
bats -
because -
behind -
between -
big -
black -
boom -
bright -
brother -
building -

built -
but -

## C

can -
can't -
carefully -
cars -
cave -
chaos -
characters -
colonies -
colony -
construction -
curious -
curiously -

## D

danger -
dangerous -
day -
days -
daytime -
different -
do -
does -
doesn't -
dog -

dog's -
don't -

## E

eight -
Einstein -
end -
engineer -
engineers -
epilogue -
especially -
everyone -
everything -
everywhere -
excellent -
explosion -
explosions -
explosives -
eyes -

## F

fast -
faster -
fiction -
five -
flies -
fly -
flying -

**for** -
**four** -
**front** -

## G

**go** -
**goes** -
**going** -
**good** -
**grrrakka kkakkakkakka** -

## H

**had** -
**hand** -
**hands** -
**has** -
**have** -
**he** -
**he's** -
**hear** -
**hears** -
**her** -
**highway** -
**highways** -
**him** -
**his** -
**horrible** -

## I

**I** -
**I'll** -
**I'm** -
**idea** -
**ideas** -
**if** -
**important** -
**impossible** -
**in** -
**intelligent** -
**into** -
**is** -
**isn't** -
**it** -
**it's** -
**its** -

## J

**Juliana** -
**Juliana's** -

## K

**know** -

## L

**laboratory** -
**let's** -
**light** -

lights -
like -
listen -
listening -
listens -
look -
looks -
lot -

## M

machine -
machines -
man -
manager -
Mediterranean -
Merlin -
metal -
microchip -
money -
monsters -
more -
mountain -
mouth -
mouths -
moving -
Mr. Rich -
my -

## N

name -
need -
needed -
needs -
night -
nine -
no -
noise -
not -
now -

## O

of -
officials -
oh -
on -
one -
open -
opens -
or -
other -
others -
out -

## P

part -
people -

problem -
protect -
real -
red -
rich -
rock -
rocks -
run -
running -
runs -

## S

Salvador -
Salvador's -
say -
says -
secret -
see -
sees -
seven -
Shadow -
she -
she's -
silence -
silently -
sister -

six -
sleep -
sleeping -
small -
so -
spaces -
Spain -
special -
stop -
stops -
story -
suddenly -

## T

takes -
than -
that -
that's -
the -
their -
them -
then -
there -
there's -
they -
think -

thinking -
thinks -
three -
time -
to -
too -
total -
towards -
trapped -
tunnel -
tunnels -
two -
typical -

**V**

vampires -
very -
visit -

**W**

walking -
walks -
wall -
walls -
want -
wants -
was -
we -
well -
were -
what -
what's -
where -
white -
who -
why -
will -
with -

**Y**

yellow -
yes -
you -
you're -
your -

# THANKS

The present edition of *Juliana* is another adventure in long distance collaboration, this time between the United States, France and New Zealand. I had the opportunity to work on this translation and adaptation with three English native speakers who are experts in using Comprehensible Input based methods to teach foreign languages:

- **Anny Ewing**, based in the USA, she is a French and Spanish teacher, teacher-trainer & coach; translator, copyeditor, and founder of *Altamira Language Learning*.
- **Dr Terry Waltz**, based in the USA, she is a Mandarin Chinese teacher, teacher-trainer & coach, translator & interpreter (Mandarin, Spanish & English), author of *TPRS with Chinese characteristics* and of numerous titles of literature for language learners, and founder of *Squid for Brains*.
- **Judith Logsdon-Dubois**, based in France, is an English teacher (professeur agrégé, DEA), teacher-trainer & coach, and founder of *The Agen Workshop*.

Thank you, Anny, Terry and Judith, for bringing *Juliana* to life in English.

Margarita Pérez García, Wellington, 14 April 2019

www.ingramcontent.com/pod-product-compliance
Lightning Source LLC
Chambersburg PA
CBHW020830020526
44118CB00032B/526